Heart
Humor &
Healing

Edited by Patty Wooten, R.N.

Commune-a-key
PUBLISHING

DEDICATION

*I would like to dedicate this book to Norman Cousins,
Vera Robinson, RN EdD, and William Fry, Jr., MD.*

*Representing the perspectives of the patient, nursing and medicine,
their research has offered validity, inspiration and guidance for
all of us interested in the therapeutic value of humor.*

book. Patty writes the same way Emmett Kelly shows us humor rather than lecturing on it.

This book offers page upon page of humor, jokes and anecdotes. One page makes you laugh and the next makes you cry. The emotions are abundant, providing insight into mankind's indomitable spirit. What I liked best was the surprise of expecting a joke book and getting instead a meaningful exercise in humor the Emmett Kelly way. Nancy Nurse is a great nurse to have at your bedside... table.

> — I. Martin Grais, MD, Asst. Professor of Clinical Medicine, Northwestern University Medical School

Heart, Humor & Healing provides uplifting information that can be enjoyed in small doses. As a humor professional I heartily recommend this for anyone who's ill or in need of a respite from the stressors of life.

> — Kathleen Keller Passanisi, PT, President, New Perspectives

A happy little book that's fun to read when you're feeling good, and good medicine when you aren't having any fun. A nice gift to buy yourself for any occasion.

> — Doug Fletcher, RN, <u>Journal of Nursing Jocularity</u>

Illness or pain can keep the mind preoccupied with thoughts about oneself. But humor can free the spirit from this narrowness of focus. *Heart, Humor & Healing* is an invaluable sickbed companion.

> — E.T. (Cy) Eberhart, Hospital Chaplain

Bravo to Patty Wooten for a wonderful collection of stories and quotes that are all heart. Her book is the perfect marriage of the laughing spirit with the loving spirit.

> — Lee Glickstein, Center for the Laughing Spirit

Patty has discovered the true Heart of Humor. This book is a celebration of joy and laughter. It is a must read for all the helping professionals who want to laugh more and stress less.

> — Jim Pelley, CSP Laughter Works Seminars

WHAT OTHERS ARE SAYING ABOUT THIS BOOK

As a physician I know how important a sense of humor is. Patty Wooten gives us an excellent gift of joy and healing in her book, *Heart, Humor & Healing*. It's good for more than your heart. It will help heal your life and body.

> — Dr. Bernie Siegel, author, *Love, Medicine & Miracles; Peace, Love & Healing;* and *How to Live Between Office Visits*

As a registered nurse, I found Patty's book to be a valuable tool to inspire staff and give encouragement to patients. Every medical professional should have this book as a resource for stress reduction!

> — Leslie Gibson, RN, Mortan Plant Health System

Being a breast cancer survivor as well as a comedienne, a daily dose of humor is a must for me. Patty's book is a wonderful gift of funny stories and inspirational quotes that will lift your spirits and brighten your day. Humor has helped in my own healing process and this book brought laughter to my heart.

> — Jane Hill, BS, BCS, Comedienne and breast cancer survivor

This book is like your own seminar with Patty. She not only convinces us that laughter is good medicine, she gives us a dose of it!

> — Jan Adrian, MSW, Healing Journeys

Reading this book is like opening a treasure chest. Each quote, anecdote and guideline for combining humor with healthcare is a gem. Patty takes you from Ha-Ha to Aha! in this unique collection guaranteed to create Global Heartwarming.

> — Karen Silver, The Laughter Prescription Newsletter

As I read Patty Wooten's book, I imagined the painting of Emmett Kelly, the clown, with the sad mouth and the tear rolling down his cheek. Patty is a nurse and a professional clown named Nancy Nurse. That's not as strange a combination as it sounds as you will see from her

Whether you are a health care professional or just trying to stay healthy, this book will make your heart sing and your spirit fill with laughter and joy.

— Allen Klein, author of *The Healing Power of Humor*

This delightful volume is good medicine. Read two pages every four hours while ill, recovering from surgery or undergoing stress. Medicare should cover this prescription.

— Christian Hageseth III, MD, PC

As a professional clown, I know that "laughter is the best medicine." Keep this book at hand and give your own giggles a tune-up, or help a friend find a few more smiles!

— Cathy Gibbons, <u>Laugh-Makers Variety Arts Magazine</u>

Patty has captured many wonderful sayings, reflections and stories. Some make you laugh, others smile and a few will cause you to reflect on life's deeper meaning. I recommend this book to all those who treasure the gift of humor.

— "The Fun Nun," Sister Mary Christelle Macaluso,
RSM, PhD

Laughter is good medicine! This wonderful little book offers healthy doses to aid in the healing process.

— Vera M. Robinson, RN, EdD, author, *Humor and the Health Professions*

This book will not only make you laugh, but will move you with stories that show how humor can bubble up from the deep healing reservoir of the human spirit.

— Carol L. Montgomery, RN, PhD, author, *Healing Through Communication: The Practice of Caring*

Commune-A-Key Publishing
P.O. Box 507
Mount Shasta, CA 96067
U.S.A.

Wooten, Patty.
    Heart, humor & healing / Patty Wooten.
    p. cm.
    Includes bibliographical references and index.
    Preassigned LCCN: 94-70997.
    ISBN 1-881394-43-3

    1. Wit and humor—Therapeutic use. 2. Laughter—Therapeutic
use. 3. Mental health. 4. Health. I. Title. II. Title: Heart, humor
and healing.
BF575-L3W66 1994   158
                                        QBI94-683

        Cover design by Lightbourne Images, Ashland, OR.
    Page design by Quicksilver Productions, Mt. Shasta, CA.
        Printed by Griffin Printing, Sacramento, CA.
        Cover photo by Paul Herzoff, Emeryville, CA.

        ISBN 1-881394-43-3 $9.95 softcover

ACKNOWLEDGMENTS

So many people have helped make this book possible.

My greatest appreciation is to the authors whose quotes are contained in this book. Your insights, creativity and humor will guide, inspire and comfort others.

Many thanks to Barbara Collins RN, Malcolm MacDonald, EdD. and Jan Adrian MSW, who, ten years ago, encouraged my exploration of humor and the development of my speaking career.

To Allen Klein, my friend and mentor, for his inspiration and support.

To Lois Richter, my secretary and office manager, whose whimsical nature, creative insights and attention to detail enrich my work and keep my business running smoothly.

To Caryn Summers, my editor, who believes in my ability to communicate this message and gives me pep talks when I get discouraged.

To my dear friend Christi Bengard, who makes me laugh and reminds me to take time to play.

To my son, Ken Wooten, who brings incredible joy to my life.

And of course, to my parents, Richard and Yvonne Savercool, without whom my whole life would not have been possible.

INTRODUCTION

If you or a loved one are facing a difficult time in your life, finding a few moments to laugh may help to restore your sense of perspective and hope. This book has been created to offer patients, their families and health care providers an alternative perspective to the sometimes frightening and frustrating experience of hospitalization or the challenges of illness. It is my intention that this collection of quotes about heart, humor and healing will touch, tickle, and teach everyone who reads it.

During the many years of my nursing career, I have watched people use their sense of humor to create feelings of hope and empowerment in situations where they felt discouraged or threatened. I know that my ability to laugh has helped me cope with the pain and tragedy in my personal life, and I have witnessed the relief that laughter brings to my patients' lives.

Health care reform began years ago when health care professionals realized that treatment efforts that focused on the physical body were incomplete unless we attended to the patient's mind and spirit as well. The emotions we experience and the beliefs we hold send messages to the body which can help or hinder its healing potential. Research continues to prove the effect of attitude and emotion upon the experience of illness and the outcome of treatment.

Our sense of humor gives us an ability to find joy when faced with adversity. May these quotes help you find that joy, lift your spirits and guide you toward optimal health.

Mirth is God's medicine.

– Henry Ward Beecher

*T*he way to maximize your creativity is to cultivate as much inner joy as possible and give yourself all the permission you need to enjoy yourself fully.

— Harold Bloomfield, MD

Our attitude
is the crayons
that color our world.

– Allen Klein

*L*ife does not cease to be funny when people die any more than it ceases to be serious when people laugh.

— *George Bernard Shaw*

When my brother was two years old, it was found that he had cancer in his kidney... The cancer had spread to his lungs... There was no hope. I didn't even know it. My parents and brother knew, but no one told me. I found out from my brother. We were fooling around one night and I must have hurt him some because he said, "Be careful, I'm going to die." I'll never forget the words...

We took him to Florida as his last wish. A few weeks after we got back, he died. And that day I died some also. Well, I have accepted his death but I still can't talk about him without crying. He taught me about life. He taught me to love, no matter what, to accept things as they are and not to question them, and most importantly, that there is life after death.

— Brother of child with cancer

*B*eginning with the early dawn each day, I will radiate joy to everyone I meet. I will be mental sunshine for all who cross my path. I will burn candles of smiles in the bosoms of the joyless. Before the unfading light of my cheer, darkness will take flight.

— Paramahansa Yoganandaj

A merry heart doeth good like a medicine, but a broken spirit drieth the bones.

– Proverbs 17:22

If you take yourself
too seriously, there's a
chance you may end up
seriously ill.

— Matt Weinstein

*L*et the surgeon take care to regulate the whole regimen of the patient's life for joy and happiness. . . allow his relatives and special friends to cheer him up, and by having someone tell him jokes. . . keep up your patient's spirit by music and viols and 10-stringed psaltery. The surgeon must forbid anger, hatred and sadness in the patient, and remind him that the body grows fat from joy, and thin from sadness.

— Henry de Mondeville, Professor of Surgery (1260-1320)

*T*he creator made man able to do everything — talk, run, look and hear. He was not satisfied, though, until man could do just one thing more — and that was: LAUGH.

And so man laughed and laughed. And the creator said, "Now you are fit to live."

— Apache Myth

When we laugh, muscles are activated. When we stop laughing, these muscles relax. . . Many people with arthritis, rheumatism and other painful conditions benefit greatly from a healthy dose of laughter.

– William Fry, MD

11

I have a new philosophy. I'm going to dread only one day at a time.

— Charlie Brown

Warning signals of Terminal Seriousness:

- ♥ Persistent soreness about almost everything.
- ♥ Frequent sudden changes of molehills into mountains.
- ♥ Difficulty swallowing humor.
- ♥ Emotional constipation.

– Paul E. McGhee, PhD

*T*o laugh often and much, to win the
respect of intelligent people and the
affection of children. . . to leave the world
a bit better. . . to know even one life has
breathed easier because you have lived,
that is to have succeeded.

— Ralph Waldo Emerson

One thing I know: the only ones among you who will be truly happy are those who will have sought and found how to serve.

– Albert Schweitzer, MD

Humor is tragedy plus time.

– Carol Burnett

*L*aughter is a way of killing fear. It's fine to make awful jokes about your illness if it helps you. It's important to laugh about it.

– Betty Rollin, breast cancer survivor

Q: What would Clint Eastwood say to the dialysis nurse if he had a kidney problem?

A: Go ahead - piss me off.

— Mark Darby, RN

*B*ecause the work of physicians and nurses is stressful and often tragic, we often rename our activities or observations in a more humorous style:

♥ Minimal urine output is referred to as "bladder sweat" for which we may have to administer Lasix to "jump start the kidneys."

♥ If something goes wrong in the nursery we may state that "Meconium (baby feces) happens."

♥ A full liquid diet could be presented as "Cream of Nothing soup."

♥ The neurology unit might refer to themselves as "Brains - R - Us." The cardiac catheter team may call the angioplasty procedure "Dilating for Dollars."

— Patty Wooten, RN

A SMILE costs nothing, but gives much. It enriches those who receive, without making poorer those who give. It takes but a moment, but the memory of it sometimes lasts forever. None is so rich or mighty that he can get along without it, and none is so poor but that he can be made rich by it. A smile creates happiness in the home, fosters good will in business, and is the countersign of friendship. It brings rest to the weary, cheer to the discouraged, sunshine to the sad, and it is nature's best antidote for trouble. Yet it cannot be bought, begged, borrowed or stolen, for it is of no value to anyone until it is given away. Some people are too tired to give you a smile. Give them one of yours, as none needs a smile so much as he who has no more to give.

— Author Unknown

*H*umor can be
a way to move
from "grim and bear it"
to "grin and share it."

— Joel Goodman

21

*O*ver the years, I have encountered a surprising number of instances in which, to all appearances, patients have laughed themselves back to health, or at least have used their sense of humor as a very positive and adaptive response to their illness.

— Raymond A. Moody, Jr., MD

*I*f you can laugh at it,
you can live with it.

— Author Unknown

*E*very nurse knows:
There are two kinds of tape -
the kind that doesn't stay on
and the kind that doesn't come off.

— "Nancy Nurse"

*N*urses, in an effort to save time, will often make hastily composed notes in their patients' charts. A variety of nurses have observed these amusing comments:

♥ Patient resting in bed with visitors.
♥ Fecal heart tones heard.
♥ Large brown BM, walking down the hall.
♥ Vaginal packing out, doctor in.
♥ Patient ate half a tray while laying in skeleton traction.
♥ Discharged with prescription on foot.
♥ The patient describes chronic constipation for which she uses prune juice and hot flashes since 1976.
♥ Disappeared after bowel movement today.
♥ Her husband lives with her, sleeps with her, but is retired.

— Author Unknown

When the woes of existence beset us, we urgently seek comic relief. The more emotions we invest in a subject, the greater its potential for guffaws.

— Patch Adams, MD

In order to laugh,
you must be able to
play with your pain.

— Annette Goodheart, PhD

*D*o doctors make amnesia
patients pay in advance?

– Author Unknown

$\mathcal{M}$any nurses have shared with me the funny ways patients have misinterpreted what the physician told them about their illness:

- ♥ Fibroids of the uterus – Fireballs of the Eucharist
- ♥ Cirrhosis of the liver – Ferocious liver
- ♥ Ovarian cyst – Bavarian Cyst
- ♥ Tubal ligation – Tubal Obligation
- ♥ Varicose veins – Very close veins
- ♥ Sickle Cell anemia – Sick as Hell Anemia
- ♥ Microorganisms in my blood – Micro Orgasms in my blood
- ♥ Myocardial infarction – Mighty internal fart

– Patty Wooten, RN

I read joke books, watch funny movies and laugh. It works as a pain reliever and also helps to lift my depression. Laughter gives one a positive self image so important when your self esteem is so low through constant sickness.

– Pat Lacey, patient with Chronic Fatigue
Immune Deficiency Syndrome

*C*hoose to have fun.
Fun creates enjoyment.
Enjoyment invites participation.
Participation focuses attention.
Attention expands awareness.
Awareness promotes insight.
Insight generates knowledge.
Knowledge facilitates action.
Action yields results.

— Oswald B. Shallow

*A*t my age it's nice to have birthday parties. All my friends can stand around the cake and keep warm.

– George Burns, at age 90

*T*he seven ages of man are:
   spills,
      drills,
         thrills,
            bills,
               ills,
                  pills &
                     wills.

– Richard Needham

*H*umor reminds us of our fragility, our earthiness, our dustiness, our propensity to mess things up even when we have the best of intentions, our powerlessness apart from God.

– Cal Samra

Dear God,
  I wish you would
not make it so easy for
people to come apart.
I had 3 stitches and
a shot.

  – A child's letter to God

I was a patient in the ICU... My temperature was 106, my blood pressure was skyrocketing and my lungs filled up with fluid. I heard the doctor tell my nurse, "His wife better get here (quick) or it will be too late." I thought, "Why do these things happen to me? What did I do to deserve this?"

As if in answer, my nurse Cindy entered. . . She struck a no-nonsense pose, placed a hand on my forearm and whispered, "You are messing up my day. If you had any idea of the paperwork involved in terminations you wouldn't be screwing around like this. My shift ends soon and if you make me late for my date, I'm going to be upset."

Cindy's words yanked me from the abyss of self pity, and my 'poor me' attitude vanished. As she explained later, "Doctors, nurses, drugs and equipment are minor when compared to a patient's attitude."

After this experience, I promised myself I would laugh more often and hunt for humor in my life.

— Mike Duckworth, a cardiac surgery patient

STANDARD PROCEDURE:
Whatever the prognosis is
For better or for worse,
For updating: see the doctor
For uplifting: see the nurse.

> — Janet Henry, breast
> cancer patient

37

*P*eople tell me they feel more available to
life once they learn how to clown around.

That's what being a clown is about.
It's about touching your soul
and finally giving it room to laugh.

—Arina Isaacson

*P*ointing out the comic elements of a situation can bring a sense of proportion and perspective to what might otherwise seem an overwhelming problem.

– Harvey Mindess, PhD

Since I came to the White House, I got two hearing aids, a colon operation, skin cancer, a prostate operation, and I was shot. The damn thing is I've never felt better in my life.

– Ronald Reagan

A patient sat in the doctor's waiting room and repeated over and over "I hope I'm sick, I hope I'm sick, I hope I'm sick."

The nurse asked him why he wanted to be sick? He told her, "I'd hate to be well and feel like this."

— Author Unknown

A nurse from England was on duty in the emergency department, when a punk rocker entered. This young woman had purple hair styled into a mohawk, a variety of tattoos and strange clothing. It was determined that the patient had acute appendicitis and was scheduled for immediate surgery. When she was completely disrobed on the operating table, the staff found that her pubic hair had been dyed green and above it was a tattoo reading: "KEEP OFF THE GRASS." After the prep and the surgery, the surgeon added a small note to the dressing which said: "SORRY, HAD TO MOW THE LAWN."

— Patty Wooten, RN

S ometimes
you just need to look
reality in the eye,
and deny it.

          — Garrison Keillor

I knew a patient who had one of his legs amputated at the hip in order to save his life from bone cancer.

As he slowly healed, he developed a profound compassion for others in similar situations. He began to visit people in the hospital who had also suffered severe physical losses.

On one occasion, he visited a young singer who was so depressed about the loss of her breasts that she would not even look at him. The nurses had the radio playing, hoping to cheer her up. It was a hot day, and the young man had come in running shorts. Finally, desperate to get her attention, he unstrapped his artificial leg and began dancing around the room on his one leg, snapping his fingers to the music. She looked at him in amazement, burst out laughing, and said, "Man, if you can dance, I can sing."

— Naomi Remen, MD

THE BOOMERANG:

When a bit of sunshine hits ye,
After passing of a cloud,
When a fit of laughter gets ye,
And Ye'r spine is feeling proud,
Don't forget to up and fling it,
At a soul that's feeling blue,
For the minit that ye sling it,
It's a boomerang to you.

— Author Unknown

45

A conscientious student nurse was carefully completing her nursing intake assessment. She was interviewing an 80-year-old woman attempting to determine the severity of her illness. She asked: "Mrs. D., have you ever been bedridden?" To which the patient smiled and replied: "No dear, but I've done it in a haystack a few times."

– Patty Wooten, RN

Hope for miracles, but don't rely on one.

— Yiddish proverb

*T*hree-year-old Gabriel, was intently playing when his father began to talk to him. "Shhhh, shhhh, Daddy," Gabriel said sternly. "I'm playing and I have to listen to my imagination."

– Karilee Halo-Shames, RN, PhD

Your joy is your sorrow unmasked.
And the selfsame well from which
your laughter rises was oftentimes
filled with your tears.

— Kahlil Gibran

My father-in-law, who was dying of brain cancer, came home from a hospital stay. It was his and my mother-in-law's anniversary so I suggested that they invite a few friends over for dinner. . .

Jimmy managed to get out of bed to join us. The strain of feeding himself and the presence of guests were obviously tiring him. Knowing that he could not hear very well, my mother-in-law passed a note to me to give to him. I read it and got hysterical with laughter. She remembered what she wrote and laughed too.

The note said, "Happy Anniversary Dear. Do you want to go to bed?"

Jimmy read his wife's note, looked across the table, and with a twinkle in his eye and a smile on his face said, "I would love to dear, but we have company."

– Allen Klein

Wrinkles
should merely indicate
where the smiles have been.

– Mark Twain

Ν o sound is so pure,
so exhilarating,
so refreshing,
so infectious,
so inspiring,
as the unrestrained
laughter of a child.

– Polly Schack

If you want others to be happy,
practice compassion.
If you want to be happy,
practice compassion.

– Dalai Lama

I live by this credo: Have a little laugh at life and look around you for happiness instead of sadness. Laughter has always brought me out of unhappy situations. Even in your darkest moment, you usually can find something to laugh about if you try hard enough.

– Red Skelton

Misery comes free. Joy, fun and laughter take planning.

– C.W. Metcalf

An ability to laugh, the courage to smile, a propensity for optimism and a playful disposition are healthful frames of mind that may accelerate healing and recovery from illness.

— Robert Holden

Y ou can create the opportunity for more laughter in your life by doing the following:

♥ Remember to laugh at yourself.
♥ Cut out cartoons and post them (or share them with someone who's ill).
♥ Add captions to baby pictures, newspaper and magazine photos.
♥ Spend time in toy stores and play with or buy some of the toys.
♥ Learn a magic trick and perform it for friends.
♥ Decorate yourself with funny things like Groucho glasses, animal noses, funny hats, clown noses, funny buttons, very large sunglasses.
♥ Brighten your sick room with items like humorous posters on the ceiling, stuffed animals, funny photos, playful pillowcases, colorful mobiles, bumper stickers.
♥ Hang around people who can make you laugh and see the funny side of life.
♥ Take time to read the comics, listen to funny audio tapes or radio shows, watch funny videos or TV shows.
♥ Keep small wind-up toys, coloring books, bubbles, or fun sound makers nearby to play with.

— Patty Wooten, RN

*A*n optimist goes to the window every morning and says, "Good morning, Lord."

The pessimist goes to the window and says, "Good Lord, morning!"

— Author Unknown

*T*hen I commanded mirth
because a man hath no
better thing under the sun
than to eat, drink, and to
be merry.

– *Ecclesiastes 8:15*

*N*o matter how grouchy you're feeling,
You'll find the smile more or less healing.
It grows in a wreath
All around the front teeth,
Thus preserving the face from congealing

— Anthony Euwer

There are no language barriers
when you are smiling.

— Allen Klein

*T*ake time to work - It is the price of success.
Take time to think - It is the source of power.
Take time to play - It is the secret of perpetual youth.
Take time to read - It is the foundation of wisdom.
Take time to be friendly - It is the road to happiness.
Take time to love and be loved - It is nourishment for the soul.
Take time to share - It is too short a life to be selfish.
Take time to laugh - It is the music of the heart.
Take time to dream - It is hitching your wagon to a star.

— Author Unknown

S even days without laughter
makes one weak.

– Joel Goodman

A nurse on the hospice unit asked me to visit a dying man who, needed to talk "about death." I was exhausted but agreed to try. I walked into his room and became acutely aware that death lurked. I noticed that the man was about 6 ft. tall and weighed 80 pounds. I had never seen anyone so thin. I was scared. I put my hand out and said "Hi. The nurse asked me to talk with you about death." I smiled stupidly (What had I just said? I never talked like that.)

He looked up at me with the bluest, brightest eyes I had ever seen. He said, "Looks like you've had a pretty rough day!"

"Yes," I replied. There was silence. My eyes swelled with tears. I apologized for the way I entered the room and he interrupted me with, "It was last week I was concerned about death. I'm not anymore. Hey, why not sit down and let me tell you my favorite joke?"

Tears streamed down my face. Tears began filling his eyes. "What has 75 balls and drives old ladies crazy?"

"Oh, good Lord, what?!"

"Bingo!"

We laughed as if it were the best and finest joke either of us had ever heard — and we cried as if there were no tomorrow. I left his room knowing that I had been given a rare gift of a lifetime.

— Donna Strickland RN, MSN

I f we have experienced loss — the loss of
friends, loved ones, financial security,
dreams, or faith — we desperately need
that healing humor that comes from the
deep common bonds we all share. We need
what Garrison Keillor describes as that
chuckle that starts deep within. We need
the laughter that is so very close to tears
— our other great healing agent. We need
to remember that only if we can laugh at
ourselves, can we forgive ourselves (for
being so human) and start over — and over.

— Ellie Marek

Humor is chaos, remembered in tranquillity.

— James Thurber

"Good morning, Mr. Abercrombie," I said to a little old man in our nursing home. "It's time to get weighed."

Mr. Abercrombie looked up at me with a sudden sparkle in his eyes. "I'll say it's time," he said, "I haven't been laid in years."

— Ruth Kremer, RN

*H*umor is contagious.
Laughter is infectious.
Both are good for your health.

– William Fry, MD

I think the 11th commandment
should have been:
Laugh and be merry.
Do not take thyself too seriously.
For he who laughs, lasts.

— Vera Robinson, RN, EdD

One hospital rewrote a traditional Christmas song to reflect the service they provided.

The Twelve Days of Christmas:
    12 Doctors smiling
    11 Nurses Caring
    10 P.T.'s Rubbing
    9 Patients Healing
    8 Tongue depressors
    7 Stethoscopes
    6 Hearts A Beating
    5 Newborn Babes
    4 Volunteers
    3 Band-Aids
    2 Gaping Gowns
    and a Christmas Tree in the Lobby.

– Author Unknown

A young male patient was bleeding profusely from the vessels lining his stomach and esophagus. In addition to pumping blood into him, we'd inserted a special tube into his esophagus with a balloon on the end. We then inflated the balloon to secure the position in his esophagus and applied traction by pulling on the tube, then tied it to the face shield of a football helmet which the patient wore. The bleeding was uncontrolled for several days as the patient's condition worsened.

The nurses cared deeply for this young man. We were all sad about his imminent death. Perhaps he noticed our sadness, because one morning he called us over to the bedside, pointed at his helmet and asked: "What team am I on?" We all laughed and cried at the same time.

— Patty Wooten, RN

*L*aughing together can be a time of intimacy and communion, a time when we come forward, fully present and touch into each other's humanness and vulnerability. By joining in humor and acknowledging our oneness, we can have a profound experience of unity and cooperation. That in itself maybe one of the most profound expressions of healing energy of which we are capable.

— Barry Sultanhoff, MD

Keep away from the wisdom
that does not cry,
the philosophy
that does not laugh,
and the greatness
that does not bow before children.

— Kahil Gibran

*D*ear God,
I didn't think orange went with purple until I saw the sunset you made on Tuesday. That was cool.

– A child's letter to God

75

SECURITY UPDATED:
I have a candy in the freezer,
And a loved one in my locket,
A balance in my checkbook,
And a pain pill in my pocket.

— Janet Henry, breast cancer patient

Your ulcers
can't grow
while you're laughing.

— Author Unknown

*N*urses learn to minimize and maximize the impact of their statements as needed:

To the patient they may say, "You have a slightly abnormal heartbeat."
To a co-worker: "He has third-degree block."
To the Nursing supervisor: "How do I get a priest STAT?"

    – Kathleen Hribar, RN, MSN, CCRN

You know you're stressed out when your idea of a great snack during break is Maalox, Nuprin and coffee.

– "Nancy Nurse"

When one door of happiness closes, another opens, but often we look so long at the closed door that we do not see the one that has been opened for us.

— Helen Keller

When one door closes,
another door always
opens – but these long
hallways are a real drag.

– Bumper Snicker

*T*he head thinks, the
hands labor, but it is
the heart that laughs.

– Liz Curtis-Higgs

*C*ompassion for ourselves gives rise to the power to transform resentment into forgiveness, hatred into friendliness, and fear into respect for all beings. It allows us to extend warmth, sensitivity, and openness to the sorrows around us in a truthful and genuine way. The power of the compassionate heart, of genuine compassion, to transform the pain we encounter is extraordinary.

— Jack Kornfield

A retired nurse in her 70's was a patient in the ICU. She was alert but a bit disoriented after her surgery. In a nearby cubicle, a confused elderly male patient was having difficulty settling down. Whenever he was left alone he would shout out "Nurse, Nurse!" relentlessly.

At one point, his neighbor, the retired nurse, shouted back from her bed, "I'm busy right now, but I'll be there in a minute."

— Fran London, RN

How to Know your Patient is a Nurse

- ♥ Takes her own pulse while you get the temperature.
- ♥ Asks if she'll be NPO tonight.
- ♥ Lists her pills generically.
- ♥ Can thread an IV tubing through the armhole of a gown without making any knots.
- ♥ Brings a "Living Will" with her on admission and understands it.
- ♥ Makes her own bed - and the roommate's, too, if she can get to it.
- ♥ Takes out her own IV and foley catheter.
- ♥ Calls out suggestions to the code team when her roommate arrests.

– Nancy Burden, RN

No one imagines that a symphony is supposed to improve in quality as it goes along, or that the whole object of playing it is to reach the finale. The point of music is discovered in every moment of playing and listening to it. It is the same, I feel, with the greater part of our lives, and if we are unduly absorbed in improving them we may forget altogether to live them.

— Alan Watts

*D*ying is that process a
few minutes before death
when the brain is deprived of
oxygen: everything else is living.

— *Patch Adams, MD*

Nurses will often use humorous phrases to explain an observation so that the patient is less worried or bothered by it.

For example, if a nurse is attempting to help a patient go for a walk and the patient is slow and weak, she might comment: "It looks like the iron in your blood has turned to lead in your butt."

Or, "I think your get-up-and-go has got-up-and-went."

— Patty Wooten, RN

L aughs are exactly as honorable as tears. Laughter and tears are both responses to frustration and exhaustion, to the futility of thinking and striving anymore. I myself prefer to laugh, since there is less cleaning up to do afterward.

— Kurt Vonnegut, Jr.

We must learn to accept life and to accept ourselves, not blindly and not with conceit, but with a shrug and a smile. To accept in the end existence, not because it's just or reasonable or even satisfactory, but simply and plainly because it's all we've got.

— Harvey Mindess

*T*here ain't any
answer.
There ain't going to be any
answer.
There never has been an
answer. . .
That's the
answer.

— Gertrude Stein

E PIC OF THE BEDPAN

When I went into the hospital, I displayed a lot of guts—
I could take it, smile and like it, but the bedpan
        drove me nuts.
At nature's call, I'd call the nurse and when I called she ran
And soon I'd have my carcass parked upon that
        gosh-darn pan.
I'd lay back on my shoulders, but the leverage wasn't there,
And instead of doing something, I'd shoot
        a flock of air.
And when at last I'd get results, I'd feel around my seat,
To see if I had hit the pan or piled it
        on the sheet.
Cold sweat on my forehead as I'd feel with cautious care,
And with signs of satisfaction, find not a
        thing was there.
But now a new contortion would leave me weak and pale;
I'd have to work and twist and squirm to wipe my
        poor sore tail.

I'd raise my sitter, high mid-air, this closed the gaping span—
My shaky hand would slip, and then I'd grab that
      gosh-darn pan.
The muscles of my neck would bulge as I stood upon my head,
I'd make a few wild passes and fall weakly
      back in bed.
And when I'd ring, the nurse came in and carried off the pan—
I'd wonder why, on such a job, they didn't
      send a man.
Then finally, I'd settle down, with a sigh of great relief—
But, wait a minute! What's so warm and wet
      upon the sheet?
With a gasp of apprehension, I'd slowly raise my gown—
And there beneath my sitter would be a
      blotch of brown.
And so, as bed confinement goes, I'm a burly, big he man—
But gosh! It simply burns me up when I miss that
      gosh-darned pan.

– Author Unknown

*L*augh and the world laughs with you.
Cry and you cry alone.
Laugh alone and they lock you up!

— Steve Kissell

I used a little cuckoo clock to help cheer me up when I was in the hospital. It's hard to maintain a bummer when a little bird jumps out of a box and hoots at you every half-hour. It worked wonders for me in my own convalescence. Whenever the cuckoo would pop out of the clock I would attempt to squirt it with my water pistol. I was so successful at this that eventually the damn thing just rusted in place.

— Wavy Gravy

*L*ife itself cannot give you joy
Unless you really will it.
Life just gives you time and space,
It's up to you to fill it.

— *Chinese proverb*

Happiness makes
up in height for
what it lacks in length.

– Robert Frost

Having cansur isn't fun. In fact its the pits, but it's not all bad either. You get lots of cards and presents when you're in the hospital. You have to have cansur to get invited to go to Camp Courage.

— Jason Gaes, age 8

*J*ust because you're miserable, doesn't mean you can't enjoy your life.

— Annette Goodheart, PhD

A CLOWN'S PRAYER

Lord, as I stumble through this life, help me to create more laughter than tears, dispense more happiness than gloom, spread more cheer than despair.

Never let me become so indifferent that I will fail to see the wonder in the eyes of a child or the twinkle in the eyes of the aged.

Never let me forget that my total effort is to cheer people, make them happy and forget at least for a moment all the unpleasant things in their lives.

And, Lord, in my final moment, may I hear You whisper: "When you made My people smile, you made Me smile."

– Author Unknown

Practice random acts of kindness and senseless acts of beauty.

– Author Unknown

*P*hysicians have created humorous comments to provide comic relief:

♥ A surgeon may advise a colleague "never let the skin stand between you and a diagnosis," or,

♥ "A chance to cut is a chance to cure," or,

♥ An emergency room physician could advise a medical student, "If you arrive in the emergency room and don't know what to do, start putting in tubes until somebody arrives who does know what to do," or,

♥ "Halitosis is better than no breath at all," or,

♥ "If you don't know what drug to order, always order the drug on your pen."

The pure absurdity of these comments helps to balance the intense seriousness of their professional responsibilities.

– Rip Pfeiffer, MD

New clinical studies show there aren't any answers.

— Author Unknown

A friend of mine was caring for a very demanding patient who made continual use of her call light to complain or to make numerous unnecessary requests. The nurse's patience was wearing thin. Lunch trays had just been passed when the nurse was again called into the patient's room. The patient was very upset and pointed to her lunch tray announcing, "This is a bad potato!"

The nurse did the only reasonable thing. She picked up the potato and began spanking it, scolding: "Bad potato, Bad potato!"

— Patty Wooten, RN

There are two things that everyone must face sooner or later: a camera & reality. A smile is a big help in both instances.

— Author Unknown

The things that matter most in our lives are not fantastic or grand. They are the moments when we touch one another, when we are there in the most attentive or caring way. This simple and profound intimacy is the love that we all long for. These moments of touching and being touched become a foundation for a path with heart, and they take place in the most immediate and direct way.

— Jack Kornfield

In this life we cannot do great things. We can only do small things with great love.

– Mother Teresa

My husband and I were in a head-on car collision. We were newlyweds living by the skin of our teeth, looking at a serious disability for who knew how long. My husband got the worst of it. To start with, he broke every bone in his head. His face was so disfigured that I brought in pictures of him so the doctors would know what he was supposed to look like. I put a picture on top that I got at Universal Studios. I told the doctors very seriously that these pictures were of Jeff and I before the crash, so they would know how to make him look. . . The picture was of me with Tom Selleck. We all laughed and after that I knew we could survive anything together.

— Kathy Anderson

*A*t the height of laughter,
the universe is flung
into a kaleidoscope
of new possibilities.

– Jean Houston

B y being frequently in the company of children, we may learn to recapture the will to laugh and the laughing at will.

— Julius Gordon

When the first baby laughed for the first time, his laugh broke into a million pieces, and they all went skipping about. That was the beginning of fairies.

– J.M. Barrie

I'm a cheerful woman,
not a happy one.
A happy woman has no cares,
a cheerful one has cares,
but has learned to laugh
about them.

– Beverly Sills

*G*etting well is not the only goal. Even more important is learning to live without fear, to be at peace with life, and ultimately death.

– Bernie Siegel, MD

When you're depressed, the whole body is depressed, and it translates to the cellular level. The first objective is to get your energy up and you can do it through play. It's one of the most powerful ways of breaking up hopelessness and bringing energy into the situation.

– O. Carl Simonton, MD

Hope is the feeling you
have that the feeling
you have isn't permanent.

– Jean Kerr

A smile is a curve that sets everything straight.

– Phyllis Diller

Q: Why do codependents get off so cheap at the hospital?

A: They require no anesthesia and use only Band-Aids.

— Jann Mitchell

*L*aughter is a powerful tool in a powerless situation.

– Allen Klein

*A*t the age of 4 Morgan asked her Mom, "Does Lisa have cancer?" Her Mom said, "No." Morgan then asked her if another friend of her Mom's, Karen, had cancer. Her Mom again replied "No." Morgan continued to ask about several more of her Mom's friends. Each time her Mom replied "No." Finally, Morgan said to her Mom, "Well, Mommy, I really think you need to share."

– Robyn Wagner-Holtz

I was in costume at Sloan-Kettering Cancer Center when I was asked to visit Justin, a seven-year-old boy with multiple cancerous tumors, including one that would necessitate amputation one of his legs. I stepped into the room and Justin's intelligent eyes were wild like a caged animal. "Operation Desert Storm," he said. "They're gonna take my leg." "That's what I hear," I said, almost unable to cope with his directness. "I'm not going to be able to stop them, am I?" I shook my head no.

From that point on I think we decided to make the best of it. I asked him what he wanted to do. He said he wanted to jump up and down on the bed. I said I'd squirt anybody that tried to stop him. We talked about how it can be scary coming out of surgery when you don't know where you are right away. So I told him to choose one thing out of my bag that I would have them put on his bed after surgery so he would know he was okay. Justin picked my "Happy Crab" because, he said, "Even though it's a sad thing I have to do, it's a happy thing too."

The stretcher was wheeled into the room. Justin's eyes grew wild again. His mom and dad asked if I could go down to the OR with them. I gave Justin my squirt gun and said, "Only if Justin can cover for me." He squirted people all the way down. I think this experience is one of the most real things I have ever been through in my life. I will be forever grateful that I could be there for Justin and be a witness to his courage.

– Deborah Kaufmann, aka "Poop Deck" the clown

Some patients have difficulty understanding medical terminology. The following are definitions of some commonly used terms:

♥ Barium - what you do when treatment fails.
♥ Cesarean section - a district in Rome.
♥ Dilate - to live long.
♥ GI series - baseball game between teams of soldiers.
♥ Medical staff - a doctor's cane.
♥ Minor operation - surgery on a coal digger.
♥ Nitrate - lower than the day rate.
♥ Outpatient - a person who has fainted.
♥ Urine - opposite of you're out.
♥ Tumor - an extra pair.

— Author Unknown

*P*erhaps it is more important
to know what kind of patient
has the disease, than what kind of
disease the patient has.

— William Osler, MD

*S*ome Handy Exercises you can do right in your own home to prepare for the hospital experience:

♥ Drink a quart of Sherwin-Williams Eggshell Beige One Coat Coverage Interior Flat White #2. Then have your child stuff his Slinky down your throat.

♥ Put a real estate agent's "Open House" sign in your front yard and lie on your bed dressed in a paper napkin with straws stuck up your nose.

♥ Lay nude on the front lawn and ask the Chemlawn man to probe you with his applicator.

♥ Put your hand down the garbage disposal while practicing your smile and repeating, "Mild discomfort."

♥ Set your alarm to go off every ten minutes from 10:00 PM to 7:00 AM , at which times you will alternately puncture your wrist with a Phillips screwdriver and stab yourself with a knitting needle.

♥ Remove all actual food from the house.

♥ Urinate into an empty lipstick tube.

– Kathryn Hammer

*T*he good news is
that nothing icky
lasts forever.

– Deborah Norville

We don't laugh because we're happy—we're happy because we laugh.

– William James

*E*ver notice how in the movies, after a big
scare or good cry, a gut-busting laugh
occurs soon after? It's called comic relief.
Laughter discharges pent-up tension. And
laughing at ourselves provides respite from
the pain.

– Jann Mitchell

127

When I was a hospice nurse, many funny incidents surrounded the experience of dying. One night I was called to the home of a terminal patient at 2 AM. I could tell by his breathing that the time of death was near. His wife, grown children and I sat quietly around the bedside. At one point he stopped breathing for more than a minute. His wife stood up and announced "Well, he's finally passed."

The patient then took a long, gasping breath. Again he stopped breathing, this time for longer than two minutes. His oldest son stood up and said: "The waiting's over, Dad's finally checked out." Again the patient took a long, gasping breath. The wife then stood up and spoke defiantly: "Isn't that just like Charlie to keep us waiting?" We all laughed and were grateful for the chance to release the tension and anxiety.

— Patty Wooten, RN

Joking about death—
or anything else that
oppresses us—makes it
less frightening.

– Allen Klein

*P*layfulness is a kind of mood or attitude that you bring to your daily life. It's a predisposition to be spontaneous, and have fun at whatever you're doing. When you're playful, you find your attention being more fully engaged in what you're doing. You're better able to "be here now."

A playful attitude infuses you with a sense of joy and positive emotions. It creates a frame of mind in which you naturally and automatically find more funny things going on around you. I am convinced that cultivating your sense of playfulness is the key to learning to lighten up in the midst of stress.

– Paul McGhee, PhD

*S*imple ways to lighten up your life:

- ♥ Buy something from the humor section of the book store.
- ♥ Add cartoons to your daily planner.
- ♥ Sing in the shower. Sing in the car.
- ♥ Change your answering machine to an upbeat message.
- ♥ Do something nice for a child.
- ♥ Write something nice on a piece of paper, make an airplane out of it and send it to someone.
- ♥ Wear a children's Band-Aid on your adult boo-boos.

— Nancy Leff

My 87 year-old father-in-law was in the end stages of Alzheimer's. He was very depressed and refused to eat. I brought a cake that was decorated with a farm scene. He seemed pleased when he saw the cake on the table, and when I asked, "Would you like a piece of the back forty?"

He laughed out loud and accepted a piece of cake, and ate the frosting. When finished with that, he asked me, "Are we celebrating a birthday?"

I answered, "No, just celebrating."

He raised his cup of coffee and said with a big smile "Happy everything!"

It was gratifying to see that humor was still accessible to this gentleman who died three weeks later

— Betty O'Malley

*G*enuine humor is always kindly and gracious. It points out the weakness of humanity, but shows no contempt and leaves no sting.

— Author Unknown

*B*eyond jokes and even words, the laughing spirit is the essence of natural mirth that connects all human hearts in an unspoken universal language of gentle delight. Humor of the laughing spirit includes all human beings, is never at the expense of an individual or group, and does not depend on cleverness or wit to be understood.

We can see the laughing spirit in the eyes of each person when we say a conscious "hello," and we make the heart connection instantly. The pleasant release of tension, the relief that causes us to smile or chuckle when we feel the presence of the laughing spirit, comes from the sudden realization that we are not separate from each other after all.

— Lee Glickstein

I realize that humor isn't for everyone. It's only for people who want to have fun, enjoy life, and feel alive.

— Anne Wilson Schaef

*L*aughter makes your thymus plumper
and your circulation stronger.
Laughter stimulates your pumper,
Helps you live a little longer.

Laughter helps you keep your health
and it might increase your wealth.

So, don't let your organs shrivel,
give a smile, a laugh, a giggle!

It improves the atmosphere
and you'll spread a lot of cheer!

– Mercedes Nelson, RN

I don't mind dying
but I want to be well
until I get there.

— Sandra Crandall, RN, FNP

A lady came to the hospital to visit a friend. She had not been in a hospital for several years and felt very ignorant about the new technologies. A technician followed her onto the elevator, wheeling a large machine with tubes and wires and dials and lights that she thought might be a ventilator. "Boy, I would hate to be hooked up to that thing." she said.

"So would I," replied the technician. "It's a floor cleaning machine."

— Mark Darby, RN

Some days you're the bug, some days you're the windshield.

— Mark Knopfler, Singer/Songwriter

Summer: the season when otherwise normal adults are transformed into beach bunnies, surfer dudes, nautical experts and amusement park junkies. It's a season when families spend a lot of quality time together, in the local emergency room. The premise is simple: people take vacations to forget about work. Instead they forget about everything, including the laws of gravity and the laws of motion. So in the interest of injury prevention I offer a list of summer tips:

1) Pain is much easier to get than to get rid of.
2) You'll catch more fish with worms than your fingers.
3) The "boogy" board was invented by the Boogyman.
4) Your analyst does not qualify as protective head gear.
5) Don't drink and dive.
6) Don't dive.
7) Each year millions of people from around the world visit DisneyWorld. About half drive on the same side of the road as we do.

                          – Robin Walter, RN, BSN

It's very inconvenient to be mortal — You never know when everything may suddenly stop happening.

— Ashleigh Brilliant

*O*ne nurse told me a story about giving her patient a suppository: After explaining the rationale and administration procedure, he rolled over and I inserted it.

"Jeeez!" he exclaimed. "Did you use a broom handle?!"

"No, I had to put it up high so you wouldn't expel it."

"I guess you did!" he said, as he reached to his mouth to retrieve an imaginary suppository.

— Author Unknown

One of the best
things people can
have up their sleeve is
a funny bone!

– Richard L. Weaver II

How to Get Sicker:

♥ Think about all the awful things that could happen to you.
♥ Be depressed, self-pitying, envious and angry.
♥ Blame everyone and everything for your illness.
♥ Go to see lots of different doctors. Run from one to another, spend half your time in waiting rooms, get lots of conflicting opinions and lots of experimental drugs.
♥ Complain about your symptoms to other people who are unhappy and embittered. Reinforce each other's feelings of hopelessness.

— Steven James

What we have learned is that the immune system is strongly affected by feelings and that taking certain kinds of psychological action can affect the immune system positively. Sometimes this makes a crucial difference in how well the medical program works.

— Lawrence LeShan

Humor can be found in Zen, in the Native American cultures, in the Jewish and Hindu traditions ... and in many others. In all of them, masters, holy fools, and sages are cherished as inexhaustible sources of sanity, healing, and wholeness. Their laughter, in the words of Yuan-Wo, is "like a cool, refreshing breeze passing through the source of all things."

— Lorraine Kisly

*F*rom there to here,
and here to there,
funny things are
everywhere.

– Dr. Seuss

A nurse should be kind, speak gently, love much and laugh often.

– L. Seaman

*L*aughter is a melody,
a concert from the heart,
a tickling by the angels,
creative living art.

Laughter heals and comforts,
sometimes gentle sometimes bold.
Laughter is a freeing dance,
performed within the soul.

— Serene West

*G*ive yourself to love
if love is what you're after.
Open up your heart
to the tears and laughter
and give yourself to love.

— Kate Wolf

A path with heart will include our unique gifts and creativity. The outer expression of our heart may be to write books, to build buildings, to create ways for people to serve one another. It may be to teach or to garden, to serve food or play music. Whatever we choose, the creations of our life must be grounded in our hearts. Our love is the source of all energy to create and connect. If we act without a connection to the heart, even the greatest things in our life can become dried up, meaningless, or barren.

— Jack Kornfield

*D*uring your hospitalization, a time when you will be receiving more visitors than the Smithsonian, you will look like something the puppy coughed up. These hints will help you look your best:

♥ <u>Don't</u> wear the standard-issue hospital gown. Hospital gowns are custom-tailored to the individual patient by the same people who make one-size-fits-all panty hose. It is illegal for these gowns to meet in the back.

♥ <u>Do</u> bring along a pillowcase to wear over your head. If you must wear a hospital gown, a simple yet elegant pillowcase slipped over the face will hide your identity and shield you from the embarrassment caused by your exposed parts.

♥ <u>Do</u> bring a floor-length robe. You'll want this coverage for times when you're in a wheelchair being paraded through the visitor's lounge and onto the public elevator with your bedwear hiked up to your waist.

♥ <u>Don't</u> wear makeup. This is like spray-painting dead shrubbery green. A sickly woman with filthy hair bolting from her head, tubes up her nose and IV lines running everywhere is not improved by blue eye shadow and red lipstick.

— Kathryn Hammer

*D*ear God,
    Instead of letting people die
and having to make new ones, why
don't you just keep the ones you
got now?

    – A child's letter to God

My life is but a weaving between my Lord and me,
I cannot chose the colors, He weaveth steadily.
Sometimes He weaveth sorrow, and I in foolish pride,
Forget He sees the upper and I the underside.
Not 'til the loom is silent and the shuttles cease to fly,
Shall God unroll the canvas and explain the reason why
The dark threads are as needful in the weaver's skillful hands,
As the ones of gold and silver in the path that He has planned.

— Author Unknown

*A*s I was eating breakfast one morning I overheard two oncologists conversing. One was complaining bitterly, "You know, Bob, I just don't understand it. We used the same drugs, the same dosage, the same schedule, and the same entry criteria. Yet I got a 22 percent response rate and you got a 74 percent. That's unheard of for metastatic lung cancer. How do you do it?"

His colleague replied "We're both using Etoposide, Platino, Oncovin, and Hydroxyurea. You call yours EPOH. I tell my patients I'm giving them HOPE. As dismal as the statistics are, I emphasize that we have a chance."

— William M. Buchholz, MD

Hope sees the invisible, feels the intangible and achieves the impossible.

— Author Unknown

*P*atient: Every morning at five I have a BM.
Nurse: That's fine; what seems to be the problem?
Patient: I don't wake up until six.

— Jeanne Mueller, RN

Don't sweat the small stuff.
It's all small stuff.

— Author Unknown

It only hurts when you don't laugh. Laughter is like the valve on the pressure cooker of life. You either laugh at stuff or you end up with your brains on the ceiling. If you don't have a sense of humor, it just isn't funny anymore. I forget who said that stuff, but I'll testify to its authenticity.

—Wavy Gravy

You can turn painful situations through laughter. If you can find humor in anything — even poverty — you can survive it.

— Bill Cosby

Who ever thought up the word Mammogram? Every time I hear it, I think I'm supposed to put my {breast} in an envelope and send it to someone.

— Jan King

One out of every nine women will develop breast cancer. On April 23rd, I became a ninth woman. Ironic, isn't it? For two years, I visited the world of children struggling [with cancer] to stay alive. I observed them; I gave them a voice. But I had never lived in their neighborhood. Now I belonged there, and I strained to recall the words of these kids...

Weeks after surgery, a local anchorwoman was touting a special on women with breast cancer and said in the teaser, "There are ways to help you become a whole woman after a mastectomy." The words <u>whole woman</u> made me crazy. They were insensitive and offended me... Where do the myths get started and why are they perpetuated? Big breasts are always accompanied by single-digit IQ's. Small breasts never get asked to the prom. The part of me that is missing didn't think, laugh, or contribute a single thing to this planet. Without a breast, I still form coherent sentences and intelligent opinions. I defy anyone to read my columns and tell me which ones were written by a single-breasted writer.

– Erma Bombeck

*I*t seems that lawyers make strange dictation errors:

♥ We are refraining from providing you with copies of the medical records, which are enclosed.

♥ Mrs. Williams weighed approximately 250 pounds and was referred to a Dr. Stout.

♥ Plaintiff is claiming $125,000 in medical specials, which we believe is grossly exaggerated. If he will not submit to a medical examination, we would recommend an autopsy.

♥ Deponent states that she told the doctor of her injury to her head and was therefore referred to a urologist.

♥ The plaintiff states that she had a tubal litigation.

♥ The patient was found on the floor in the nurse.

♥ Plaintiff claims that the hospital was negligent in its care for the plaintiff, that the decedent's condition was incorrectly diagnosed, that the surgery was inadequately performed, and that improper precautions were taken to avoid internal bleeding. Other than that, she had no complaints about the hospital.

– Steve Kluger

It's been lovely but I
have to scream now.

— Author Unknown

165

*T*o survive we need dollars,
   but to really live we need
some common sense:
Sense of humor,
   Sense of purpose,
      Sense of presence,
         Sense of self, and a
            Sense of joy.

— *Sandy Ritz, RN, MSN*

Our biological senses (sight, sound, taste, touch and smell) were designed to provide us with the tools to gather information and provide safety from our environment.

It may stand to reason that the loss of a sense of humor is the most significant form of sensory deprivation.

— Leslie Gibson, RN

I was doing a sexual history on my patient at the time of her Pap test. I asked my 80-year-old if she was sexually active, and she replied, "Well, not active, active - not every night!!!"

– Sandra Crandall, RN, FNP

I've got herpes, I've got AIDS –Guess you can say I'm an incurable romantic.

– J.S., AIDS patient

169

We helpers deserve to nurture ourselves as well as those we care for. Some caregivers think that to sacrifice and suffer is spiritual. I believe this might be called "spiritual anorexia."

— Caryn Summers, RN

You have reached the
Codependent Hotline.

If you want to save the world, press 1.
If you want to rescue your family, press 2.
If you want to change your partner, press 3.
If no one appreciates you, press 4.
If you do not have a touch tone phone, stay
on the line and an operator will speak with
you after she's through with the really
important people.

– Jann Mitchell

*T*hose who do not know
how to weep
with their whole heart
don't know
how to laugh either.

— Golda Meir

Humor is the great thing,
the saving thing, after
all, the minute it crops up all
our hardnesses yield, all our
irritations and resentments
flit away, and a sunny spirit
takes their place.

— Mark Twain

STRESS MANAGEMENT TECHNIQUES:

- ♥ Write a memo congratulating yourself for being so wonderful.
- ♥ Answer a highly technical question in your best Donald Duck voice.
- ♥ Take an eight hour lunch break.
- ♥ For a quiet evening, play a blank cassette at full volume.
- ♥ Pretend that you're someone else.
- ♥ Eat gelatin with chopsticks.
- ♥ Pretend that you're still in control.
- ♥ Ring somebody's doorbell and run away.

— Donna Strickland, RN, MS

Give yourself
        permission
to take an intermission.

– Helen Lerner

... *P*lay is essential for health. In this sense, play is defined as any activity which tends to produce the emotions of joy or the experience we call having fun. So each person must define play for himself. Our energy and our will to live are increased by play. Play improves the quality of life and makes it richer. It lifts us out of despair and increases our <u>wish</u> to live. It increases the energy needed to mobilize the <u>will</u> to live as well.

— O. Carl Simonton, MD

A clown is like an aspirin, only he works twice as fast.

– Groucho Marx

Humor does not
diminish pain –
it makes the space
around it get bigger.

– Allen Klein

When I was in the hospital I had a "We" nurse. She began each sentence with: "How are we today?" "We need to have a bath." This really irritated me so I decided to play a little joke on her.

One day she brought in a specimen cup and requested a urine sample. After she left, I poured my apple juice into the cup. When she returned for the specimen, she observed it and noted: "My, we're a little cloudy today, aren't we."

I asked to see it and then removed the lid, said: "Yep, better run it through again," and drank it. The look of shock on her face was priceless.

– Norman Cousins

179

ANATOMY OF A NURSE'S POCKET:

Lunch money, life savers, kelly clamp,
bandage scissors, roll of tape,
pen light, stethoscope, alcohol swabs,
tongue blades, cups, ammonia capsules,
straws, pen, pencil, list of patients,
Band-aids, aspirin, lipstick,
pocket guide of nursing diagnosis,
breath mints, knock `em dead perfume,
map to happy hour.

— RN Concepts

Nurses have soooo much to do. Everybody is always calling, "Nurse help me." "Nurse turn me." "Nurse feed me." We are running around like a mother with too many hungry children (like one big breast to the world), saying: "Have a little suck of this." I figure that's why it's called "nursing."

— "Nancy Nurse"

It is a fact of life that we find ourselves in unpleasant demoralizing situations which we can neither escape nor control. We can keep our morale and spirits high by using both "coping" and "hoping" humor.

Coping humor laughs at the hopelessness in our situation. It gives us the courage to hang in there, but it does not bring hope.

The uniqueness of hoping humor lies in its acceptance of life with all its dichotomies, contradictions and incon-gruities. It celebrates the hope in human life. From one comes courage, from the other comes inspiration.

– Cy Eberhart

H ope: Tomorrow's veneer over today's disappointment.

— Evan Esar

Sometimes I think it is like this:
    God has a TV set
and God watches us on it.
Whenever I think I'm being watched,
I always sing and dance
and do a commercial for myself.

— "Edith Ann" by Jane Wagner

*T*o tragedy belongs guilt
and judgment; to comedy
love and grace.

— Conrad Hyers

I have seen what a laugh can do. It can transform almost unbearable tears into something bearable, even hopeful.

– Bob Hope

Q: What do you call a person with recurrent lymphoma?

A: A Lymphomaniac.

— Told at a cancer support group

Nurses will often complain that the physician's handwriting is difficult to read. This problem has been partially rectified by providing doctors with dictation equipment. However, occasionally they push the wrong button, use jargon or misplace the modifiers. The following are actual phrases collected by medical transcriptionists:

♥ Both the patient and the nurse herself reported passing flatus.

♥ By the time she was admitted to the hospital, her rapid heart had stopped, and she was feeling much better.

♥ Skin: Somewhat pale but present.

♥ Patient left his white blood cells at another hospital.

♥ She had a miscarriage at the age of four months.

♥ Husband also relates severe menstrual bleeding the past two periods.

- Physician has been following the patient's breast for six years.
- Discharge status: Alive but without permission.
- The nursing home where the patient lives was noted to sputter, cough and run a fever.
- The patient was seen about four weeks ago by a physician with a urethral drip.
- She left the hospital nursing her baby and draining clear urine.
- Healthy appearing, decrepit 69 year-old white female, mentally alert but forgetful.
- The patient had an unsteady gait while standing on one foot removing his pants.
- Patient stated that if she would lie down, within two or three minutes something would come across her abdomen and knock her up.
- We have had no major deaths using this technique.

— Authors Unknown

*L*ife can be wildly tragic at times, and I've had my share. But whatever happens to you, you have to keep a slightly comic attitude. In the final analysis, {don't} forget to laugh.

— Katherine Hepburn

When I was a student nurse, I was working at a hospital in San Francisco. The main street in San Francisco is called Market Street and originates in the hills and travels down to the wharf. As I was about to bathe my patient, I noticed a large scar from a previous surgery. The scar began just below her breastline and continued to her pubic region. As I asked her about it, she said, "Oh I call that Market Street."
Surprised, I asked her why.
She said, "Because it goes from Twin Peaks all the way to the waterfront."

— Patty Wooten, RN

191

*C*omedy is the main weapon we have against "The Horror." With it we can strike a blow at death itself. Or, at least, poke a hole in the pretentious notion that there is something dignified about it.

—John Callahan, Cartoonist and quadriplegic

*C*ancer is probably the most unfunny thing in the world, but I'm a comedienne, and even cancer couldn't stop me from seeing humor in what I went through.

– Gilda Radner

When someone has a personal phone call during a hectic time in our emergency room, we use the code, "Dr. Jones is on the phone." This provides discretion when one is with a patient. One busy night, Christie's nine-year-old son called for the second time that night. Christie was treating a man with a minor laceration right outside the nurse's station, so it was easy to attract her attention.

"Oh Christie, Dr. Jones is calling." I said. Christie asked the man to keep pressure on the wound, and headed for the phone.

The patient overheard when Christie snarled, "What did I tell you mister? You get into that tub immediately!" and slammed down the phone. She never noticed her patient's wide eyes. But he did follow her every instruction.

— Vince Moravek, RN

When people are
smiling they are
most receptive to almost
anything you want to
teach them.

– Allen Funt

A List of Books about New Age Topics:

♥ <u>There's No Mind, Never Mind - and Zen Some</u>, by Roshi Alzheimer.

♥ <u>The Midget Psychic Who Escaped from Prison</u>, by a small medium at large.

♥ <u>I Never Metaphysics I Didn't Like</u>, by Will Tulku Rogers.

♥ <u>A Knife Thrower's Guide to Acupuncture</u>, by Guy Fat Fang.

♥ <u>Everybody Needs Samadhi Sometime</u>, by Paramahansa Yogananda Parlez-Vous?

♥ <u>The Egyptian Book of Dead Jokes</u>, by Pharaoh Hohotep.

♥ <u>Don't Fall Off a Limb</u>, by Surely Deranged.

— Joseph Jochmans

Humor is a rich and versatile source of power — a spiritual resource very like prayer.

— Marilyn R. Chandler

*T*o encourage patients to take deep breaths after surgery, nurses or respiratory therapists will teach the patient to use inspirometers. Several years ago, a popular model included a chamber with three plastic balls, which when the patient blew into the mouthpiece hard enough the balls would rise to the top of the chamber.

The young male respiratory therapist had been working with 85-year-old Mrs. M. every hour, and she was growing weary. As he entered the room for the ninth time, the patient announced: "Looky here, sonny. You can just blow your own balls!"

— Patty Wooten, RN

You know you're getting older when you stoop to tie your shoes and you ask yourself, "What else can I do while I'm down here?"

— George Burns

Nightly Ritual

I prop my wig up on the dresser,
And tuck my prosthesis beneath,
And I thank God
I still go to bed
With my man
And my very own teeth.

— Janet Henry, breast
cancer patient

Your ability to laugh
and be silly can help
you thrive in adversity by
accessing joy in absurdity.

– Donna Strickland, RN, MSN

201

Q: What do you get when you kiss a canary?

A: Chirpes. It's a canarial disease. But don't worry, it's tweetable.

— Shannon Lawrence, RN

I had just finished applying a condom catheter to my slightly confused 70-year-old patient, when he scolded me: "Does your mother know what you do for a living?"

— Patty Wooten, RN

Aorta Take Care of Myself

We who joined the Mended Hearts
Can shyly boast of mended parts.
There's courage derring do to rate
When heart trained surgeons operate.
And of all the patients
We're the stars,
When it comes to boasting scars.
But here's what seems like heck to me:
The lowly hemmroidectomy.
Painful, itchy, done up-ended,
Can they boast of what's been mended?
And what a lousy deal they got
Joining Mended You Know What!

— Duncan Stewart

Any day above ground
is a good day.

— Author Unknown

I spell relief, L-A-U-G-H:

L is for <u>let go</u>. If we are holding on to anything - anger, upset, frustration and we don't let go we become stressed out.

A is for <u>attitude</u>. Things are the way they are. It is our attitude that makes the difference.

U is for <u>Y-O-U.</u> You are the only one who can change your attitude.

G is for <u>Go do it</u>. Begin adding humor to situations.

H is for <u>humor eyes</u> and <u>humor ears</u>. Humor is all around but we must look and listen for it.

– Allen Klein

*T*en minutes of genuine belly laughter had an anesthetic effect and would give me at least two hours of pain-free sleep.

— Norman Cousins

The more one suffers,
the more, I believe, one has
a sense of the comic. It is only
by the deepest suffering that
one acquires the authority in
the art of the comic.

– Soren Kierkegaard

Q : What's the worst thing about having a heart-lung transplant?

A : You have to cough up somebody else's sputum.

— Marti Murray, RN

*F*or what, after all, is the laughter a good clown brings us but the giddiness that comes from suddenly seeing, as if from a cosmic viewpoint, the absurdity of what the mighty are up to?

For that moment, we taste the sanity of divine madness, and become, for as long as the joke lasts, fools of God.

— Theodore Rozak

On his death bed, Oscar Wilde looked around the room and said: "This wallpaper is terrible. One of us has to go."

— Oscar Wilde

To laugh is to risk appearing the fool.
To weep is to risk appearing sentimental.
To reach out to someone is to risk
    involvement.
To expose feelings is to risk exposing your
    true self.
To place your ideas, your dreams before a
    crowd is to risk their loss.
To love is to risk not being loved in return.
To live is to risk despair.
To try is to risk failure.
But risks must be taken, because the
    greatest hazard in life is to risk nothing.

— Author Unknown

If you're gonna walk on thin ice, you may as well dance.

— Jessie Winchester

Not one shred of
evidence supports
the notion that life is
serious.

— Author Unknown

Kid saying the pledge of allegiance: "I led the pigeons to the flag, of the United States and a Miracle — One nation and a vegetable."

— Roger Langley

If laughter is as contagious as it is said to be, then let's start an epidemic. Or perhaps we need doctors by the thousands to prescribe regular doses of humor.

Though this 'Great Laughter Cure' may not be a panacea, it is reassuring to learn, in these days of painful and expensive medical therapies, that laughter is medicinal and the only side effects are pleasurable.

— Robert Ornstein, PhD,
& David Sobel, MD

A person without a sense of humor is like a wagon without springs — jolted by every pebble in the road.

— Henry Ward Beecher

*E*verything can be taken from a man but one thing: the last of the human freedoms - to choose one's attitude in any given situation, even if only for a few seconds.

— Victor Frankl

I got to be a little bit crazy, 'cause it keeps me from going insane.

– Country Western Song

You know what happens when
  you get angry?
First, your face gets just like a fist.
Then your heart gets like a bunch
of bees that flies up and stings
your brain in the front.
Your eyes are like two dark clouds
looking for trouble.
Your blood is like a tornado.
And then you have bad weather
inside your body.

— "Edith Ann" by Jane Wagner

A smile is a light
on your face
that lets people know
your heart is home.

— Author unknown

The witch doctor succeeds for the same reason all the rest of us succeed. Each patient carries his own doctor inside him. They come to us not knowing that truth. We are at our best when we give the doctor who resides within each patient a chance to go to work.

— Albert Schweitzer, MD

There is no medicine like hope, no incentive so great, and no tonics so powerful as expectation of something better tomorrow.

— Orion Swett Marden

A sense of humor can help you overlook the unattractive, tolerate the unpleasant, cope with the unexpected, and smile through the unbearable.

— Moshe Waldoks

*T*he song collection you've been waiting for—your favorite tunes by the hottest all-nurse singing groups:

"Sugar in the Morning"- by The Dipsticks.
"The Wayward Wind"- by The Flatulents.
"Never My Love"- by The Frigidaires.
"I've Got You Under My Skin"- by The
　　Scabies.
"Great Balls of Fire"- by Orchitis and
　　The Mumps.

－ Steve Tiger

225

*A*ttitude is everything in recovery from cancer. You gotta have 'tude if you expect to take a licking and come back ticking.

Tumor humor is not warm and friendly, it's scrappy and sometimes nasty and tasteless, a sort of chemotherapy for the spirit - necessary but {not always} nice.

The most important part of a fighting attitude is humor, because it keeps you loose.

— Robert Lipsyte, a cancer patient

*L*ife is a tragedy when seen in close-up, but a comedy in long shot.

— Charles Chaplin

I was working in the emergency room during my third year as a resident in cardiology. The ambulance had brought a man into the hospital in full cardiac arrest. While the rest of the team was busy with the Code, I went out to interview the wife about the possible causes.

She explained to me: "Well, we was making love, and he just started shakin' and shakin' and turnin' blue. I couldn't figure out if he was comin' or goin.' Finally, I figured out he was goin' so I called 911."

— Martin Grais, MD

W arning: Humor may be hazardous to your illness.

— Author Unknown

I was preparing to leave the hospital when one of the doctors gave me some last minute instructions. He told me to wait two weeks before I had sex and six weeks before I drove a car. Or was it the other way around? I was still a little foggy and the entire discussion confused me, so I just promised him that I wouldn't have sex and drive at the same time and let it go at that.

— Lewis Grizzard

*D*on't deny the diagnosis. Try to defy the verdict.

— Norman Cousins

What's new in New Age thought and therapy?

- ♥ Reincarnation Life Insurance
- ♥ Karma Donors
- ♥ Extraterrestrial Abductees Support Group
- ♥ Tibetan Boozism: Out on a Binge
- ♥ Great Book of the Near-Dead
- ♥ Eating Your Way to Enlightenment: Pigging Out on the Path
- ♥ Do-It-Yourself Firewalking
- ♥ Macroneurotics
- ♥ Acupuncher
- ♥ Crystal Enemas: Light Up the Darkness
- ♥ Mozart Flower Remedies
- ♥ The Harmonica Virgins

— Chris Kilham

We are all here for a spell. Get all the good laughs you can.

—Will Rogers

Sorrow or a wound can heal, allowing us to grow into our fullest, most compassionate iden-tity, our greatness of heart. When we truly come to terms with sorrow, a great and unshakable joy is born in our heart.

— Jack Kornfield

The art of the clown is more profound than we think. . . It is the comic mirror of tragedy and the tragic mirror of comedy.

– Andre Suares

When we love and laugh with our patient, we elevate the highest degree of healing, which is inner peace.

— Leslie Gibson

According to Buddhist scriptures, compassion is the "quivering of the pure heart" when we have allowed ourselves to be touched by the pain of life. The knowledge that we can do this and survive helps us to awaken the greatness of our heart. With greatness of heart, we can sustain a presence in the midst of life's suffering, in the midst of life's fleeting impermanence.

— Jack Kornfield

Surround yourself with
people who bring happiness
into your life,
things that you love, fresh air,
laughter, good food;
and make plans for tomorrow.

— Jane Hill, breast cancer
survivor and comedienne

If needles were noodles, I'd cook up ca-boodles
So no one would ever get hurt!

If I was the head of this hospital here
I'd bring in a dump truck of sterilized dirt.

I'd say "Let the kids play! Do whatever they say!
And give them whatever they want for dessert!"

If doctors and nurses would rock to-and-fro
We could sit on their heads and say "Giddy-up-Go!"

And ride them around and collect all the pills
Then pile them up into sliding-down hills.

Take off the stethoscopes! Chuck the white coats!
Slide down the pills using bedpans for boats!

– Peter Alsop & Penny Pefley, RN

*A*nything that restores a sense of control to a patient can be a profound aid to a physician in treating serious illness. That sense of control is more than a mere mood or attitude, and may well be a vital pathway between the brain, the endocrine system and the immune system.

— Norman Cousins

Did you ever notice that the bigger the dressing you put on a patient, the more satisfied they are?

— "Nancy Nurse"

*T*he hardest thing you can do is smile when you are ill, in pain, or depressed. But this no-cost remedy is a necessary first half-step if you are to start on the road to recovery.

— Allen Klein

*T*he rezin I wanted to write
a book about having cansur
is because every book I read
about kids with cansur they
always die. If you get cansur
don't be scared, cause lots of
people get over having cansur
and grow up without dying.

– Jason Gaes

A chuckle a day may not keep the doctor away, but it sure does make those times in life's waiting room a little more bearable.

— Anne Wilson Schaef

*L*et's not forget the healing power of humor, for ourselves, our patients and our colleagues.

Humor lightens the burden of a difficult day, unhappy situation, or unpreventable mistake.

— Helene Nawrocki, RN, MSN

Happiness is like a butterfly.
The more you chase it,
the more it will elude you.
But if you turn your attention
to other things, it comes and
softly sits on your shoulder.

— Author Unknown

JOY
is the flag you fly
when the Prince of Peace
is in residence
within your heart.

— Wilfred Peterson

. . . *Laughter* serves as a blocking agent. Like a bullet-proof vest, it may help protect you against the ravages of negative emotion that can assault you in disease.

— Norman Cousins

Years after my father died, I was helping my mother sort through his belongings in the closet and I came across Dad's medical bag. Inside there was a note—instructions from one doctor to another about the care of patients in his absence. Most of the notes identified routine prescriptions and treatments, but there was one that jumped off the page. It read simply: "Mrs. Stevens is not sick, but she doesn't know it. I just sit with her, hold her hand and listen." It was at this moment that I discovered what real medicine was all about.

— Polly Schack

A good laugh
lifts your spirits,
touches your heart
and enriches your life.

– Jim Pelley

A hospital telephone operator told me that one day an older gentleman called inquiring what time visiting hours were.

When she informed him that it was 11 AM to 8 PM, he answered in dismay, "Oh my, I don't think I can stay THAT long!"

— Betty O'Malley

*S*omething special happens
when people laugh together
over something genuinely funny,
and not hurtful to anyone. It's
like a magic rain that showers
down feelings of safety and
belonging to a group.

— Mary Jane Belfie

H

e deserves
Paradise
who makes his
companions laugh.

– Mohammed

In traditional Navajo Indian culture, the child is viewed as the ultimate gift, a precious gift that must never be abused. The First Laugh ceremony ensures that an infant is constantly watched over and kept in a cradle board until the child laughs for the first time. This moment marks the child's birth as a social being. The member of the family or friend of the family who makes the baby laugh must then provide a celebration in honor of the child.

— Navaho First Laugh Story

$\mathcal{P}$EACE
starts with a smile.

— Mother Teresa

We have lived through the era when happiness was a warm puppy,

and the era when happiness was a dry martini,

and now we have come to the era when happiness is "Knowing what your uterus looks like."

— Nora Ephron

I have a card with diagrams of how to do a breast exam hanging in my shower. Usually I leave the picture side facing the wall. However one day the cleaning lady left it turned outward and my 7-year-old son Jake saw it and asked me what it was for. Without going into much detail, I told him it was there to remind me to do something every month and to show me how to do it. Jake replied, "Mama, I can't believe you don't know how to wash your boobs."

– Peggy Johnson

I believe that play is the
beginning of creativity.
I believe that laughter is the only
cure for grief and fear.
I believe that humor is the bond
that can unite us all.

— Ellie Marek

*L*aughter is not at all a bad beginning for a friendship, and it is by far the best ending for one.

– Oscar Wilde

AN ESSAY ON GOD

One of God's main jobs is making people. He makes these to put in place of the ones that die, so there will be enough people to take care of things here on earth.

God's second most important job is listening to prayers. An awful lot of this goes on, as some people, like preachers, pray other times besides bedtime.

God doesn't have time to listen to the radio or TV on account of this. God sees everything and hears everything and is everywhere. Which keeps Him pretty busy.

Jesus is God's Son. He used to do all the hard work, like walking on water and doing miracles and trying to teach people about

God who didn't want to learn. They finally got tired of His preaching to them and they crucified Him. God appreciated everything He had done and all His hard work on earth so God told Him He didn't have to go out on the road any more.

Now He helps His Father out by listening to prayers and seeing which things are important for God to take care of and which ones He can take care of Himself without having to bother God. Like a secretary only more important, of course.

You can pray anytime you want and they are sure to hear you because they've got it worked out so one of them is on duty all the time. And that's why I believe in God.

— Danny Dutton, age 8

Any nurse who can provide the patient with a sense of hopefulness has the true gift of healing.

– Patty Wooten, RN

*E*ach human being possesses a beautiful system for fighting disease. This system provides the body with cancer-fighting cells - cells that can crush cancer cells or poison them one by one with the body's own chemotherapy. This system works better when the patient is relatively free of depression, which is what a strong will to live and a blazing determination can help to do. When we add these inner resources to the resources of medical science, we're reaching out for the best.

— Norman Cousins

The laughing experience transforms the moment and lingers, creating a happy feeling and prompting a sense of oneness and contentment often reflected in personal descriptions of health.

— Rosemarie Rizzo Parse, RN, PhD, FAAN

*T*he most wasted day
  of all is that on which
we have not laughed.

— Sebastian Chamfort

No pessimist ever discovered
the secrets of the stars, or
sailed to an uncharted land,
or opened a new Heaven to
the human spirit.

— Helen Keller

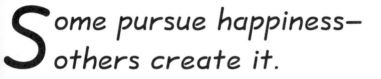

*S*ome pursue happiness—
others create it.

– Author Unknown

Most of us have a significant fear of losing control and equate its loss with some type of failure. Using humor as a coping skill requires that we give up some of that immediate control, step back from a seemingly overwhelming situation, and laugh at ourselves. This occasional relinquishment of control can be more than a temporary relief; it can empower us by putting us back in touch with ourselves, allowing us to re-engage with a renewed sense of self.

— Donna Strickland, RN, MSN

I live
in another dimension,
but I have a summer home
in reality.

– Author Unknown

I don't get depressed —
I grow a tumor.

— Woody Allen

We must take responsibility for our happiness and stop blaming and directing control outside of ourselves. Grab hold of all that you are. Discover new and different aspects of yourself and life – Through a happy, positive set of glasses – They are there, waiting for you to put them on.

– Helene Nawrocki, RN, MSN

If a person is gloomy, he should read a joke book, or fix his mind and memory on the funniest thing that ever happened to him or to someone else. And while this advice may shock the conventional members of society, it will heal the bruised heart, renew courage and shorten the duration of the malady, whatever it may be.

— George Wood, MD
& E.H. Ruddock, MD, 1890.

In spite of the cost of living it is still popular.

— J.L. Peter

If we consider the frequent relief's we receive from laughter, and how often it breaks the gloom which is apt to depress the mind, one would take care not to grow too wise for so great a pleasure of life.

— Joseph Addison

Clown and guru are a single identity: the satiric and sublime side of the same higher vision of life.

— Theodore Rozak

275

Nurses are called
Angels of Mercy
because they are expected
to do everything on a wing
and a prayer.

– Patty Wooten, RN

Medicine consists of keeping
the patient comfortable,
while nature takes its course.

— Voltaire

I see humor as food. I don't think that the only time people should eat food is when they're ill. An adequate share of humor and laughter represent an essential part of the diet for the healthy person.

— Norman Cousins

P

eople crave laughter as if it were an essential amino acid.

— Patch Adams, MD

H
umor is the prelude to faith, and laughter is the beginning of prayer.

— Reinhold Niebuhr

Dear God,
Here's a poem.
I love you because you give
Us what we need to live.
But I wish you would tell me why
You made it so we have to die.

— A child's letter to God

281

*T*ragedy and comedy are
but two aspects of what
is real, and whether we see
the tragic or the humorous is
a matter of perspective.

— *Arnold Beisser*

It's important to know
the difference between
Humor and Odor.

Humor is when you
shift your wit — odor is
the other way around.
It's your choice!

— "Nancy Nurse"

283

INDEX OF TOPICS

INDEX OF AUTHORS

REFERENCES

Every attempt has been made to identify the sources. Where the source is unknown, this author gladly invites information which will appear in future editions of this book, provided written notification is received.

Adams, Patch & Maureen Mylander. *Gesundheit!* Rochester, VT: Healing Arts Press, 1993.

Alsop, Peter & Bill Harley. *In the Hospital.* Moose School Records, Topanga, CA.

Bombeck, Erma. *Redbook Magazine.* Hearst Corporation. October, 1992.

Brilliant, Ashleigh. *I May Not Be Perfect, But Certain Parts of Me Are Excellent.* Santa Barbara, CA: Woodbridge Press, 1979.

Buchholz, William. <u>Western Journal of Western Medicine</u>. Vol. 148, p. 69. 1988.

Callahan, John. *Don't Worry, He Won't Get Far on Foot.* New York, NY: Vintage Books, 1990.

Cousins, Norman. *Anatomy of an Illness.* New York, NY: W.W. Norton, 1979.

Cousins, Norman. *Head First: the Biology of Hope.* New York, NY: Dutton Signet, 1989.

Curtis-Higgs, Liz. *One Size Fits All.* Nashville, TN: Thomas Nelson Publishing, 1993.

Eberhart, Cy. *In the Presence of Humor: A Guide to the Humorous Life.* Salem, OR.

Frankl, Viktor E. *Man's Search for Meaning.* New York, NY: Pocket Books, 1963.

Fry, William F. "Laughter and Health", *Encyclopedia Britannica: Medical and Health Annals.* p. 259-262. USA, 1984.

Funt, Allen. *Candid Camera: All-Time Funniest Moments.* Monterey, CA: Allen Funt Productions, Inc., 1993.

Gaes, Jason. *My Book for Kids with Cansur.* Aberdeen, SD: Melius Publishing Corporation, 1987.

Gibran, Kahlil. *The Prophet.* New York, NY: Alfred A. Knopf, Inc., 1923.

Gibson, Leslie. *Laughter: The Universal Language.* Dunedin, FL: 1991.

Goodheart, Annette. *Laughter Therapy: How to Laugh about Everything in Your Life That Isn't Really Funny.* Santa Barbara, CA: Less Stress Press, 1994.

Goodman, Joel. *Laughing Matters.* Saratoga Springs, NY: Humor Project.

Gorree, Georges & Barbier, Jean. *The Love of Christ: Spiritual Counsels from Mother Teresa of Calcutta.* New York, NY: Harper & Row, 1982.

Grizzard, Lewis. *They Tore Out My Heart and Stomped that Sucker Flat.* New York, NY: Warner Books, 1982.

Hammer, Kathryn. *And How Are We Feeling Today?* Chicago, IL: Contemporary Books, Inc., 1993.

Hample, Stuart & Marshall, Eric. *Children's Letters to God.* New York, NY: Workman Publishing, 1991.

Henry, Janet. *Surviving the Cure.* Cleveland, OH: Cope Inc., 1984.

Holden, Robert. *Laughter: The Best Medicine.* London: Thornson Publishers, 1993.

Houston, Jean in Goodheart, A. *Laughter Therapy*, p. 120. Santa Barbara, CA: Less Stress Press, 1994.

Hyers, Conrad. *The Comic Vision and the Christian Faith.* New York, NY: Pilgrim Press, 1981.

Jochmans, Joseph in C. Kilham. *In Search of the New Age.* Rochester, VT: Destiny Books, 1988.

Kaufmann, Deborah. "Send in the Clowns" in <u>American Association of Therapeutic Humor</u>, Vol. 7, No. 3, May 1993.

Kilham, Chris. *In Search of the New Age.* Rochester, VT: Destiny Books, 1988.

King, Jan. *Hormones from Hell.* Los Angeles, CA: CCC Publications, 1990.

Kissell, Steve. *Surviving Life with Laughter.* Norfolk, VA: Mirthworks, 1994.

Klein, Allen. *Healing Power of Humor.* Los Angeles, CA: Tarcher Publisher, 1989.

Kluger, Steve. *Lawyers Say the Darndest Things.* New York, NY: Ballantine Books, 1990.

Kornfield, Jack. *A Path with Heart.* New York, NY: Bantam Books, 1993.

Leff, Nancy. *Life: A Laffing Matter.* Los Angeles, CA, 1992.

LeShan, Lawrence. *Cancer as a Turning Point.* New York, NY: Plume Books, 1990.

McGhee, Paul. *How to Develop Your Sense of Humor.* Dubuque, IA: Kendall-Hunt Publishers, 1994.

Meir, Golda in Goodheart, A. *Laughter Therapy*, p. 77. Santa Barbara, CA: Less Stress Press, 1994.

Metcalf, C.W. *Lighten Up.* Reading, MA: Addison-Wesley, 1993.

Mindess, H. *Laughter and Liberation.* Los Angeles, CA: Nash Publishing, 1971.

Mitchell, Jann. *Codependent for Sure.* Kansas City, MO: Parkside Pubishers, 1992.

Nawrocki, Helene. *Nurse's Book of Courage.* Newton, PA: Center for Nursing Excellence, 1993.

Nelson, Mercedes in Goodheart, A. *Laughter Therapy*, p. 81. Santa Barbara, CA: Less Stress Press, 1994.

O'Malley, Betty. *Levity for Longevity*, and *Medical Mirth*. Davidson, MI.

Ornstein, Robert & Sobel, David. *Healthy Pleasures*. New York, NY: Addison-Wesley Publishing, 1989.

Paulson, Terry. *Making Humor Work*. Los Altos, CA: Crisp Publishng, 1989.

Pfeiffer, Rip. *A Chance to Cut is a Chance to Cure*. Mobile, AL.

Radner, Gilda. *It's Always Something*. New York, NY: Avon Books, 1990.

Rizzo Parse, Rosemarie. "The Experience of Laughter", <u>Nursing Science Quarterly</u>. Vol. 6 (1), p. 39. 1993.

Robinson, V.M. *Humor and the Health Professions*. Thorofare, NJ: C.B. Slack, 1990.

Rollin, Betty. *First You Cry*. New York, NY: Harper-Collins, 1990.

Samra, Cal. *The Joyful Christ*. San Francisco, CA: Harper & Row Publishing, 1986.

Siegel, Bernie. *Love, Medicine, and Miracles*. New York, NY: Harper & Row, 1986.

Sills, Beverly in Goodheart, A. *Laughter Therapy*, p. 31. Santa Barbara, CA: Less Stress Press, 1994.

Simonton, O. Carl. *Getting Well Again*. New York, NY: Bantam Books, 1978.

Strickland, Donna. *Laughter Matters*. Denver, CO: 1992.

Summers, Caryn. *Caregiver, Caretaker*. Mt. Shasta, CA: Commune-A-Key Publishing, 1992.

Vonnegut, Kurt Jr. in Goodheart, A. *Laughter Therapy*, p. 32. Santa Barbara, CA: Less Stress Press, 1994.

Wagner, Jane. *Edith Ann—My Life so Far*. New York, NY: Hyperion, 1994.

Wavy Gravy. *Something Good for a Change*. New York, NY: St. Martin's Press, 1992.

Weinstein, Matthew. *Playfair*. San Luis Obispo, CA: Impact Publishers, 1980.

West, Serene. *Daily Word*. Unity Village, MO: Unity Press, 1993.

Wolf, Kate. *Give Yourself to Love*. Los Angeles, CA: Rhino Records, 1983.

DIRECTORY OF HUMOR RESOURCES

American Association for Therapeutic Humor. 222 S. Meramec, Ste. 303, St. Louis, MO 63105. (314) 863-6232. Networking source for application of humor in professional settings. Quarterly newsletter.

Center for the Laughing Spirit. Lee Glickstein. 2078 21st Ave., San Francisco, CA 94116. (415) 731-6640. Authentic public speaking & tapes on healthy laughter.

Funny Times. P.O. Box 18530, Cleveland Heights, OH 44118. (216) 371-8600. Monthly newspaper with cartoons and humor about current events.

Humor and Health Newsletter. Joseph Dunn, Editor. P.O. Box 16814, Jackson, MS. (601) 932-1873.

Jest for the Health of It! Patty Wooten, RN. P.O. Box 4040. Davis, CA 95617-4040. (916) 758-3826. Nurse Humorist and Clown. Workshops, keynotes, comedy for your health.

Journal of Nursing Jocularity. P.O. Box 40416, Mesa, AZ 85274-0416. (602) 835-6165.

Joyful Noiseletter. Fellowship of Merry Christians, P.O. Box 895, Portage, MI 49081-0895. (800) 877-2757.

Keep Laughing to Keep Healthy. Jane Hill. 3941 So. "E" Bristol St., Suite 337, Santa Ana, CA 92707. (714) 546-2339. Comedienne & breast cancer survivor presenting workshops on humor and health.

Laughline Newsletter. Ellie Marek, Editor. P.O. Box 32071, Phoenix, AZ 85064. (602) 870-1399.

Laughter Prescription Newsletter. Karen Silver, Editor. 970 Shore Crest Road, Carlsbad, CA 92009.

Laughter Works Newsletter. Jim Pelley, Editor. P.O. Box 1076, Fair Oaks, CA 95628. (916) 863-1592.

Mirth, Magic and Mending. Robin Walter. 5 Belair South Parkway, Ste. 109, Bel Air, MD. (410) 893-7433. Catalog of comedy resources for patients and health professionals.

Planet Mirth. Polly Schack. 5411 Pheasant Dr., Sacramento, CA 95822. (916) 444-6934. Humor consultant, presentations on humor in the workplace.

San Francisco Clown School. Arina Isaacson. 1000 Prague St., San Francisco, CA 94112. (415) 587-3301. Clown training and character development.

The HUMOR Project. Joel Goodman, Director. 110 Spring St., Saratoga Springs, NY 12866. (518) 587-8770. Publishes *Laughing Matters*, a quarterly journal, and a catalog of humor books.

Whole Mirth Catalog. 1034 Page Street, San Francisco, CA 94117. (415) 431-1913. Humorous items, toys, gags, books.

ABOUT THE AUTHOR

Patty Wooten has been a nurse since she was two, and has practiced professionally since 1969. She has worked in clinical areas including critical care, long term care and home care. Patty writes articles about humor and health and has created a video with Norman Cousins and Alan Funt about the healing power of humor.

Founder of "Jest for the Health of It Seminars," Patty is a nurse humorist and an internationally recognized leader on the subject of the healing power of humor. Patty and her wacky character, "Nancy Nurse," have amused over 70,000 health care professionals from Bakersfield to Boston to the BBC. She is a dynamic, knowledgeable and sensitive speaker. She is also hilariously funny.

You may contact Patty at:

Jest for the Health of It!
P.O. Box 4040
Davis, CA 95617-4040
(916) 758-3826
e-mail: jestpatty@mother.com

294

ORDER FORM

Need copies for your friend? You may find books published by
Commune-A-Key at your local bookstore or you may order directly.

TITLE	QTY	TOTAL
Caregiver, Caretaker: From Dysfunctional to Authentic Service in Nursing. by Caryn Summers. Essential reading for helpers who tend to care for others before caring for themselves. $16.95 each.		
Inspirations for Caregivers. A classic selection of inspirational quotes collected by Caryn Summers on the motives and rewards for giving care to others. $8.95 each.		
Inspirations for Caregivers: Music and Thoughts. Caryn Summers reads the best quotes from *Inspirations for Caregivers*, accompanied by original music by Douglas York. $10.95 each.		
Circle of Health: Recovery Through the Medicine Wheel. by Caryn Summers. This personal growth book combines mythology, symbols, Native American tradition and psychology with twelve-step recovery tools. $12.95 each.		
the Girl, the Rock and the Water. by Caryn Summers. A mythological journey of our inner child to safety, trust and freedom. Read by the author. Includes watercolor illustrations, soundtrack, and workbook. $19.95 each.		
Heart, Humor & Healing. by Patty Wooten, RN. A delightful collection of inspiring, fun-filled and laughter provoking quotes designed to promote healing in the patient as well as the caregiver. $8.95 each.		

Mail this form with your check or money order payable to: **Commune-A-Key Publishing** P.O. Box 507 Mount Shasta, CA 96067 **1-800-983-0600**	SUBTOTAL _____ Shipping & handling: $3.00 first item, plus $1.25 each additional item. _____ Calif. residents add 7.25% sales tax. _____ TOTAL $ ENCLOSED _____

Name _____ Phone _____

Address _____

City _____ State _____ Zip _____